W9-AUD-987

Armored Vehicles

Kate Riggs

CREATIVE EDUCATION • CREATIVE PAPERBACKS

Published by Creative Education and Creative Paperbacks
P.O. Box 227, Mankato, Minnesota 56002
Creative Education and Creative Paperbacks
are imprints of The Creative Company
www.thecreativecompany.us

Design by Ellen Huber; production by Blue Design
Art direction by Rita Marshall
Printed in the United States of America

Photographs by Corbis (Shane A. Cuomo/US Army/Reuters), Dreamstime (Goce Ristesk), Flickr (The U.S. Army), Getty Images (VANDERLEI ALMEIDA), iStockphoto (breckeni, ewg3D, JaiGieEse), Shutterstock (Creativa Images, OlegDoroshin, yuri4u80)

Library of Congress Cataloging-in-Publication Data
Riggs, Kate.
Armored vehicles / Kate Riggs.
p. cm. — (Seedlings)
Includes index.
Summary: A kindergarten-level introduction to armored vehicles, covering their crew, weapons, role in battle, and such defining features as their wheels.
ISBN 978-1-60818-659-4 (hardcover)
ISBN 978-1-62832-244-6 (pbk)
ISBN 978-1-56660-673-8 (eBook)
1. Armored vehicles, Military—Juvenile literature. I. Title.

UG446.5.R544 2015
623.74'75—dc23 2015007402

CCSS: RI.K.1, 2, 3, 4, 5, 6, 7; RI.1.1, 2, 3, 4, 5, 6, 7; RF.K.1, 3; RF.1.1

First Edition HC 9 8 7 6 5 4 3 2 1
First Edition PBK 9 8 7 6 5 4 3 2 1

TABLE OF CONTENTS

UB 02207

Time to move!

Armored vehicles carry troops onto battlefields. They go where tanks (above) go.

Fighting vehicles do not have as much armor as tanks.

But they can hold more people.

Soldiers inside the vehicle can fire weapons.

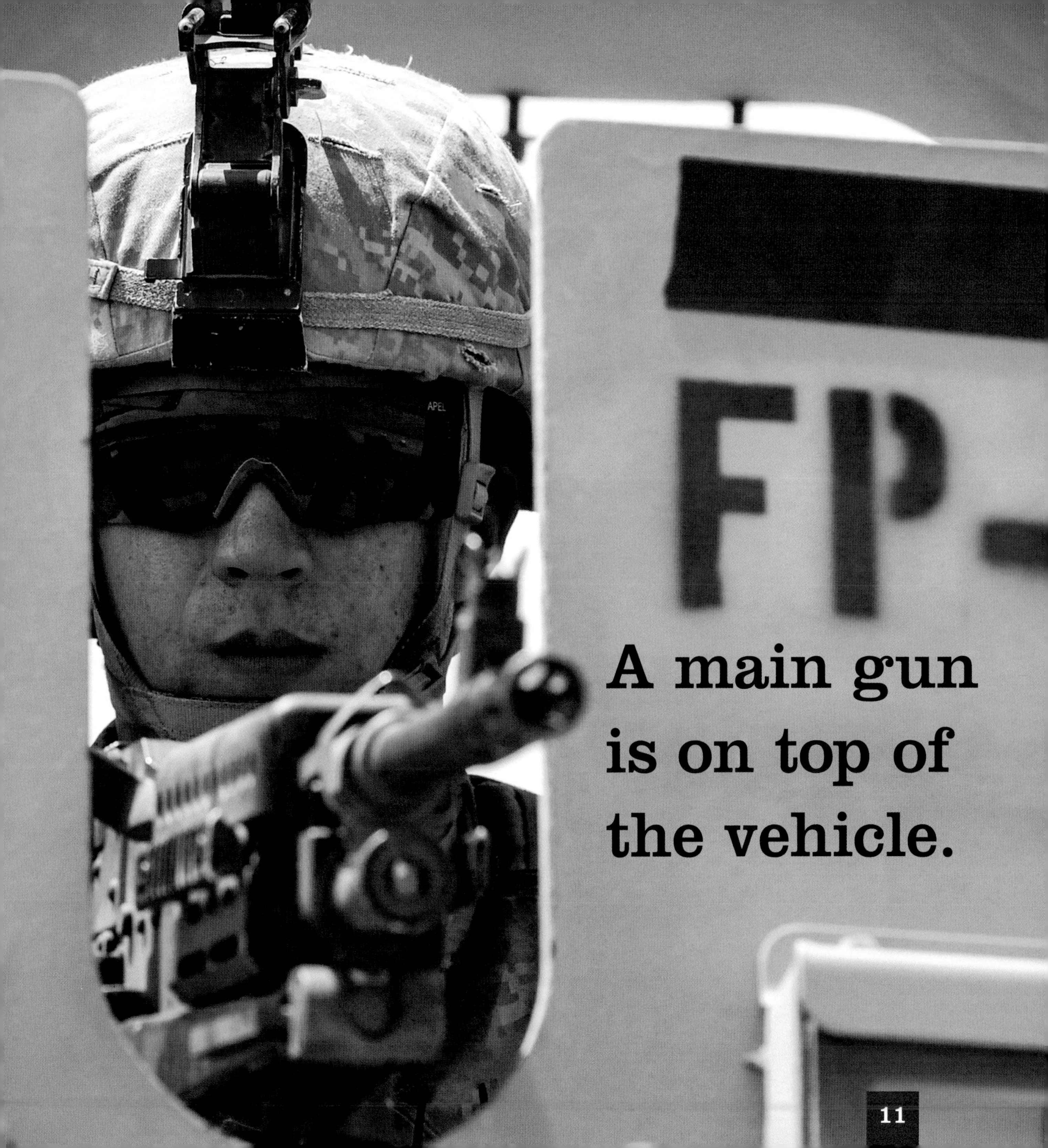

A main gun is on top of the vehicle.

One person drives the vehicle.

Another keeps a lookout for anything dangerous.

Some fighting vehicles have eight wheels. Others have more wheels and **tracks**.

LT
346

An armored vehicle carries fighters to a new place.

It drives over rough ground. It tries to keep people safe.

Go, armored vehicle, go!

Picture an Armored Vehicle

gun

track

wheel

Words to Know

armored: describing a metal covering that keeps something safe

tracks: big, strong belts that go around a vehicle's wheels

weapons: things like guns or bombs used to guard or hurt others

Read More

Alvarez, Carlos. *Strykers*. Minneapolis: Bellwether Media, 2011.

David, Jack. *M2A2 Bradleys*. Minneapolis: Bellwether Media, 2009.

Websites

Army Coloring Pages
http://www.hellokids.com/r_709/coloring-pages/transportation-coloring-pages/army-vehicles-coloring-pages
Print out a picture of an armored vehicle to color, or color it online.

U.S. Army Vehicles
http://www.goarmy.com/army-videos.sch-Army%20Vehicles.html
Watch videos about the Stryker and other fighting vehicles.

Note: Every effort has been made to ensure that the websites listed above are suitable for children, that they have educational value, and that they contain no inappropriate material. However, because of the nature of the Internet, it is impossible to guarantee that these sites will remain active indefinitely or that their contents will not be altered.

Index